I really tried not to write about you

Lina Geiger

I really tried not to write about you

Lina Geiger

Bibliografische Information der Deutschen Nationalbibliothek: Die Deutsche Nationalbibliothek verzeichnet diese Publikation in der Deutschen Nationalbibliografie; detaillierte bibliografische Daten sind im Internet über dnb.dnb.de abrufbar.

© 2022 Lina Geiger

Herstellung und Verlag: BoD – Books on Demand, Norderstedt

ISBN: 978-3-7568-7407-1

About her

(this is ~~not~~ a love story)

And no matter how mushroom I give you in my heart.. it's never enough.

She said she really loves fire and burning shit from time to time...

You know what?

Just give me a few more months and I'll change that. Because literally I'm the fire in person and (as everyone else I've ever met) she won't be able to stand me.

Yesterday I was sad.

I missed you. Not because we haven't seen a long time. But because we saw each other and knew it would be the last time. Maybe not the last time we would see each other but definitely the last time we saw one another with open eyes. With our hearts. Definitely the last time we shared our dreams and fears and the last time we trusted each other. And this made me so fucking sad. I sat down and took my own hand - and I imagined it was your hand. That calmed me.

We're strangers now.

Again.

Okay. I see.

~~You hate me.~~

I can imagine exactly one situation where I'd like her to shut up. If we'd watch the moon together I would need her to be quiet for some time because I appreciate looking at the moon together but I need a few seconds where I pray to the moon and where I'm able to drown in her beauty. That's it. And after a short moment she could talk again. As much as she wants to. And then I'd take time to drown in her way of being beautiful.

*Can I please come and stay a while in your mind?
Because I am tired of my brain and I need to get out
of this head for a while. Just share your thoughts
with me and hug me with your words until I am full
of you.*

Would you do that for me?

I'm not immune to how she looks.

I'm not immune to how she thinks.

I'm not immune to how she speaks.

I'm not immune to how she smells.

I'm not immune to her.

Guess it's over now.

Of course I would absolutely love it if she fell for me.
And yes, I sometimes hope for her to fall in love
with me. I dream about it and I think my favorite
love story is ours by far, even though this is no love
story. But no matter how much I miss the feeling of
being loved. And no matter how much I wish that
she'd love me, too. No matter how often I fantasize
about us living the most adorable love story ever. I
am always so fucking thankful that I am in love with
her. That it's not the other way round. Every single
moment I thank god that I am able to give love. To
feel love.

Because no matter how much I want to be loved…
Showing love makes me happier I guess.

The thing is you don't need skin contact to be tangled in one another. You don't need to actually touch each other to be in touch. We didn't touch for a long time and even though I never felt her I was so fucking close to her. We shared our dreams and fears and that made us so close to each other that no skin contact could compare to that. So no, it's not always about sex and touching physically. It's about the souls that tangle around each other and blend together. Touching her soul without touching her skin was so damn personal and intimate... sex couldn't compare to that.

Anyway I love touching her physically because it feels like touching the Milky Way but that's not the point here.

How can I blame you for watching me fall down instead of catching me up when I knew from the very beginning that you wouldn't help me.

How can I be mad at you for not listening to me when no one ever actually heard my words.

How could I ask for you to hear my silence when you're not even able to hear me while I'm screaming.

How can I be sad about you thinking bad of me when it was me who told you my darkest secrets.

How can I ask for your time while we are living in different worlds.

~~How can I blame you for watching me fall down instead of catching me up when I knew from the very beginning that you wouldn't help me.~~

If I had to choose between her body and her brain... I'd choose her brain.

Sure she's sexy and aesthetic but let me tell you her mind is way more attractive and I crave her mind and soul so much more than her body.

So for me it's not the shell but what's inside of her.

One of the reasons I fell in love with her is probably the one that when I started freaking out and when things got complicated she stayed. In moments where everyone else was leaving me and no one even tried to stay… in these moments she was by my side. She stepped out of her way and made it clear that she wants me in her life. She told me she won't leave me and she stayed. And maybe she actually wants me in her life. I'd like that.

Date idea:

You.

&

Me.

That's it.

The both of us.

Are you in?

I am absolutely sure that yesterday I knew way more than I know today.

I had thoughts in my mind but now I remain thoughtless.

I had visions, but they're invisible now.

I felt love, but I am out of love right now.

I knew your smell, but the only thing I am able to smell right now is the body spray you always use, which I bought to comfort myself when you're not around.

I saw things that made me smile, but today I am blind.

I heard your laugher, but all I can hear right now is silence.

And I felt you, but all I can sense right now is the cold blade on my skin and it'll give way to the feeling of my warm blood soon.

Fuck. Fuck. **Fuck. Fuck. Fuck.** Fuck. Fuck. Fuck. Fuck. Fuck. Fuck. Fuck.
Fuck. Fuck. **Fuck.** Fuck. Fuck. Fuck. Fuck. Fuck. Fuck. Fuck. Fuck. Fuck.
Fuck. Fuck. **Fuck. Fuck.** Fuck. Fuck. Fuck. Fuck. Fuck. Fuck. Fuck. Fuck.
Fuck. Fuck. **Fuck.** Fuck. Fuck. Fuck. Fuck. Fuck. Fuck. Fuck. Fuck. Fuck.
Fuck. Fuck. **Fuck.** Fuck. Fuck. Fuck. Fuck. Fuck. Fuck. Fuck. Fuck. Fuck.
Fuck. Fuck. **Fuck.** Fuck. Fuck. Fuck. Fuck. Fuck. Fuck. Fuck. Fuck. Fuck.

Fuck. Fuck. **Fuck.** Fuck. **Fuck.** Fuck. Fuck. Fuck. Fuck. Fuck. Fuck. Fuck.
Fuck. Fuck. **Fuck.** Fuck. **Fuck.** Fuck. Fuck. Fuck. Fuck. Fuck. Fuck. Fuck.
Fuck. Fuck. **Fuck.** Fuck. **Fuck.** Fuck. Fuck. Fuck. Fuck. Fuck. Fuck. Fuck.
Fuck. Fuck. **Fuck.** Fuck. **Fuck.** Fuck. Fuck. Fuck. Fuck. Fuck. Fuck. Fuck.
Fuck. Fuck. **Fuck.** Fuck. **Fuck.** Fuck. Fuck. Fuck. Fuck. Fuck. Fuck. Fuck.
Fuck. Fuck. **Fuck. Fuck. Fuck.** Fuck. Fuck. Fuck. Fuck. Fuck. Fuck. Fuck.

Fuck. Fuck. **Fuck. Fuck. Fuck.** Fuck. Fuck. Fuck. Fuck. Fuck. Fuck. Fuck.
Fuck. Fuck. **Fuck.** Fuck. Fuck. Fuck. Fuck. Fuck. Fuck. Fuck. Fuck. Fuck.
Fuck. Fuck. **Fuck.** Fuck. Fuck. Fuck. Fuck. Fuck. Fuck. Fuck. Fuck. Fuck.
Fuck. Fuck. **Fuck.** Fuck. Fuck. Fuck. Fuck. Fuck. Fuck. Fuck. Fuck. Fuck.
Fuck. Fuck. **Fuck.** Fuck. Fuck. Fuck. Fuck. Fuck. Fuck. Fuck. Fuck. Fuck.
Fuck. Fuck. **Fuck. Fuck. Fuck.** Fuck. Fuck. Fuck. Fuck. Fuck. Fuck. Fuck.

Fuck. Fuck. **Fuck.** Fuck. **Fuck.** Fuck. Fuck. Fuck. Fuck. Fuck. Fuck. Fuck.
Fuck. Fuck. **Fuck.** Fuck. **Fuck.** Fuck. Fuck. Fuck. Fuck. Fuck. Fuck. Fuck.
Fuck. Fuck. **Fuck. Fuck.** Fuck. Fuck. Fuck. Fuck. Fuck. Fuck. Fuck. Fuck.
Fuck. Fuck. **Fuck.** Fuck. **Fuck.** Fuck. Fuck. Fuck. Fuck. Fuck. Fuck. Fuck.
Fuck. Fuck. **Fuck.** Fuck. Fuck. **Fuck.** Fuck. Fuck. Fuck. Fuck. Fuck. Fuck.
Fuck. Fuck. **Fuck.** Fuck. Fuck. **Fuck.** Fuck. Fuck. Fuck. Fuck. Fuck. Fuck.

What I said: *You can call me anytime.*

What I meant: *You can call me anytime. And by that I really mean anytime. You can call me no matter if the sun or the moon shines. You can call me no matter if you're too tired to speak at all or if you're talkative as fuck. You can call me while you're crying or screaming or whatever the fuck you feel like at this moment. You can call me anytime and I hope you do. Because I don't care if you're simply saying good night or if you need a long talk about your fears and hopes. I'm always happy to hear you and I'd always listen to you. Please let me be there for you.*

What she understood: *You can call me when you're at your best but please don't show me your weak and destroyed self. I am going to disappoint you just like anyone else you've ever met. So better don't call me at all.*

I hope one day she'll kill me with a knife or gun. Better now than later. Because if not she'll kill me with her lack of affection. And with her heart. With her kind way of thinking and living. With her lovely soul. With her fucked up mind. With her weird thoughts. With her broken voice. With her smell. With everything she doesn't likes about herself. With everything what makes her her.

She's so pure, so raw, so kind. I never met anyone like her. She's loyal and lovely and weird and fucked up and complicated and so... you know. Herself. I love her. Can't even explain how much I adore her.

It's just.

Her.

It's her.

And at the end of the day I come home to you and I know everything will be okay. Because with you next to me I'm always pretty fine.

I love her and it's killing me softly.

Instead of waiting for the right time to say something nice you should say it now.

I'll go first:

You all are amazing and lovable.

Please don't ever doubt your worth.

You all matter most.

And now I'm going to tell her how important she is. Because why wait? The time is now.

They say how much you love yourself next to someone shows if the person is the right one. If ever I loved myself it was next to her. Too bad she's not around often. And our time will be over soon I guess. She'll move on and leave me behind. Just as everyone does. But anyone else doesn't count. It's about her.

Let me make one thing clear..

If she said taste me *I'd tear down her clothes, put
her on a desk, go down on my knees and lick her. I
swear to god nothing could stop me and afterwards
I would kiss her and help her getting dressed again.
Or if she'd like it I'd let her lay down on my chest
and pet her hair while she slowly falls asleep.*

*Sorry but there's no other way to handle the
situation.*

No matter how short the time will be that I am blessed to spend with her I will carry her around with me forever. She'll never leave my heart. Parts of her will always be with me.

Me: :(

*She: *exists**

Me: :)

I like you.

*I like you in a way where I'd absolutely be okay with
you pushing me against a wall and kissing me
aggressively. I'd also be okay with you kissing me
gently on my head while hugging me. And I'd also
be okay with simply holding hands during our walks.*

*Actually I don't care how you touch me, but please
touch me. In any way. Because I really like it. It
comforts me. It makes me feel loved and it feels like
a million shooting stars run down my whole body
and explode somewhere in my stomach into a
beautiful and sparkling firework made of stardust.*

Okay, but hear me out... her voice.

I'd like to kiss her lips.

I'd like to kiss her neck.

I'd like to kiss her hairs.

I'd like to kiss her hips.

I'd like to kiss her fingertips.

I'd like to kiss her face.

I'd like to kiss her legs.

I'd like to kiss her tattoos.

I'd like to kiss her scars.

I'd like to kiss her everywhere she's insecure about.

Places I wouldn't like to kiss her:

- not found -

I wish I could fall asleep next to you.

When I think about her in an intimate way it's not that I fantasize about us fucking in any way possible. It's about hugging her and gently kissing her. It's about us holding hands and feeling each other. I'm sorry but if I can't have this with her, I don't want to fuck her either.

Name a thing that is cuter than her.

She broke my heart. But now I am able to see my surrounding again. She took all of my time and I didn't care because it was her. Silly me.

I want to be able to tell you how much I like you without being afraid of you freaking out. Because that's what happened every time I tried to be honest about my feelings.

*Instead of texting me you could also call me…
'Cause then I'd hear your voice and sweetie, I
appreciate it so much more to hear you than to read
from you.*

She's crazy. I love her.

When I met her for the first time, she appealed my eyes. And a long time I loved her for being fucking beautiful, sexy and aesthetic.. I couldn't easily forget my feelings for her and it wasn't fucking easy accepting that I won't have her, not even as a friend. But life went on. And I followed.

But damn. Now I get to know her closer nearly every day and damn. Damn. DAMN. I no longer love her for being attractive. I love her heart. Her inner twisted mind. I love her way of thinking. Her way of talking. Of writing. I crave seeing the way she tries to explain her fucked up mind. The way she stumbles through life. All I wanna hear is her freaking smoky and dark laugher. Her big smile while being sarcastic. I wanna know how her day was. I need to know that she's okay and safe. This love is fucking deep and I'm gonna drown in it. And I'm looking forward for it to happen. `Cause this is the only fucking ocean I wanna swim in.
Damn. Damn. Damn.
Sorry but gotta say it again.
Damn.

Time flies by when I'm with her and I never feel bored.

Guess I'll keep her.

If she lets me.

She stepped out of her way and made it obvious that she kinda wants me in her life while kinda risking her good reputation because of meeting me private. Kinda like it. Kinda hate it because I don't want her to get problems. Complicated world. And also easy as fuck.

We like each other.

End of story.

Kinda.

I like her.

She likes me.

But we ain't fucking yet.

Honestly I don't know why.

I could sleep better if she'd say good night to me...

When I look at her it's not that everything else seems dark and blurry… it's more like she lightens up even the darkest parts.

Tonight I had a dream where I could lay next to you while you were telling me with passion, humility and kindness from your inner demons. You showed me your tattoos and even in my dream, where everything should be possible, I wasn't able to touch you. Because I were afraid of what I would feel when our skins collide. I was afraid of hurting you. I didn't want to destroy what we had. Even though I don't know what that was. We sat there for hours and afterwards we went out and observed the night sky.

You can't just touch my fucking soul and leave.

Whenever she calls me sweetie my heart kinda forgets how to beat...

There's nothing I crave more than this teeny tiny word, these seven letters, spoken by her in that melodic, smoky and pleasant voice.

I miss that little weirdo.

I always miss people who are perfectly okay with not seeing me.

Next time I should fall for someone who actually likes me.

When I look at the night sky I think about you.

While you're looking at the same stars but thinking of someone else.

Tragedy.

They say you always have to be ready to say goodbye to anything and anyone.

I'm not ready to leave you.

Please don't go when I haven't found a way to live without you. Please don't go before I figured out how my heart is supposed to beat without you. Please don't go before my brain drank enough to not feel and recognize your loss.

Please don't go before I am ready.

She is made of moonlight and a hint of rainbow glitter.

I hope she'll call me if she ever can't sleep at night. But I'm afraid that I am not the person she wanna talk to late at night when she's questioning everything. I'm pretty sure that I am not her night person. You know what I mean? The person you miss at night, the one you wanna see when you'd kill any other person you'd see in that moment. The one who's voice could make you sleepy even though you thought your mind would never ever let you sleep again. The one who could stay in silence on the phone with you and you wouldn't feel alone or lost. Anyway, I hope I am her night person. And she could call me anytime. No matter how late, no matter how long we didn't speak. I would stay on the phone as long as she wants me to.

Is it love or is it stupidity?

Actually, I don't care. It is what it is.

And if only I helped you to see the world a little bit different for a teeny tiny moment, I am pleased.

I looked at her like she's my sun and she looked at me like I am the next problem she won't get rid off.

I told her that I missed her today. And I know it's kinda pathetic and dumb. But I also know that life is short and nobody knows what will happen tomorrow...

And we're all a little bit too hurtful instead of being too kind.

And we're all a little bit too private and shy when it's time to let our hearts speak.

*So yes, I am pathetic and I am dumb.
But god is my witness I tried to be kind and I cared about her feelings and fuck, I did the freaking right thing.*

*So instead of calling me an idiot you could also ask yourself why you did hurt her in the past.
Why you don't tell her you miss her.
Why you chose to ignore her instead.*

I'm gonna tell you something.

Fuck you.

*Tonight I'll tell the moon about you. And maybe
she'll tell me about the sun.*

I guess my way of loving you will forever be me missing you.

Great for you, because you don't want me to stick around you.

*Daydreaming. Nice and deadly. Which is also nice.
Because I'm interested in all kinds of death.*

It's funny.

To me you are everything and we are my favorite love story.

But to you I am a burden and we are a weird friendship.

Vanilla, coffee, lavender, a hint of sage.. passion, art, aesthetic, safety, home, mystic.. that's what she smells like.

Okay but how am I supposed to do what my heart wants if there are a million shredded parts of it and all of them are wanting something different..?

<u>*Things I'd like to ask her (but I don't) :*</u>

Who's on your mind while looking at the night sky?

How can I be there for you?

Do you actually like me, or am I just an interesting project?

Did you ever dream about me? What was it about?

Would you leave me if I'd tell you how much I like you?

Am I too complicated for you?

If you had to describe me, what would it be?

Will you ever understand me? Or at least do you try to?

Am I annoying?

How am I supposed to act next to you?

What am I to you?

What is my role in your life?

<u>Things I'd like to ask her (but I don't) :</u>

What's my name in your phone?

How do you feel next to me?

How do you want to be loved?

Are you your true self while spending time with me?

Can we watch movies and hold hands?

Did you ever lie to me? When and why?

What makes you you?

What is art in your eyes?

What's some free therapy for you?

What's your chapter that you don't read out loud?

What are you afraid to lose?

What do you want?

The end came way faster than I thought it would but somehow it's better this way. So I won't make her world too complicated. She won't suffer from me any longer. Maybe it's better for her and maybe it's better for me, too. Because I adore life more when I am with her and maybe my path won't include being happy and alive.
So fuck it.

The end.

~~I'm sorry.~~
~~I know you don't want me to love you...~~

It was a pleasure to call you my friend.

Fuck